Copyright © 2025 by Simon Chiatante
All Right Reserved

Foreword: Prof. Zhang Guangkui
Afterword: Prof. Matteo Convertino
Illustrations: Rocco Caloro
Graphic Design: Giovanni Capoccia & Luca Martelli

Second Edition: July 2025
Published by Subway Dharma Collective

Simon Chiatante

Respiro

Metropolitan Haiku

Subway Dharma Collective

For
Mario & Nuccio Chiatante

Each
Silently true to themselves

Haiku and Urban Romanticism

"Respiro" is Italian for "breath". It carries connotations of breathing — a sigh, or even a moment of relief or pause, a sense of renewal, introspection, a fleeting moment of awareness. As the poet Simon Chiatante himself explains: "By breathing, we are able to see life's truth and beauty, even in the midst of metropolitan chaos and the speed of modernity". This sentiment resonates deeply throughout the collection, as Simon transforms Shenzhen's urban rhythm into a poetic canvas in search of "truth and beauty".

Another key term that shapes this collection is "haiku", which comes from Japanese and evolved from the opening verse of "renga", a genre of collaborative linked verse poetry, and it was Masaoka Shiki (1867–1902) who designated the opening verse as the independent poetic form known today as haiku. Japanese haiku consist of 17 syllables arranged in a 5–7–5 pattern, typically structured with Japanese kana sounds (one kana equals one sound or syllable). Haiku often incorporates a kigo (seasonal word) to indicate the time of year, and a kireji (cutting word), which serves as a particle or auxiliary verb to create a pause or shift in meaning. The Haiku form has had a profound influence on the West. In 1913, American poet Ezra Pound (1885–1972), one of the most prominent representatives of the Imagist movement, published the first English haiku "In a Station of the Metro". This poem is not only a representative work of Imagism, but it is perhaps the pinnacle of English haiku to date. Yet, Pound chose not to strictly adhere to the traditional structure, thus opening the way for a tradition on non-Japanese haiku, adhering to their ethos but not necessarily to their structure.

Having read Simon Chiatante's poetry collection multiple times, I was immediately reminded of "Haiku in English: The First Hundred Years", the most authoritative anthology of English haiku published to date. Naturally, Ezra Pound's "In a Station of the Metro" is included in this collection. Simon's haiku style bears a strong resemblance to the haiku featured in this anthology.

What sets Simon apart, though, is his careful adherence to the traditional Japanese haiku ideals of clarity and tidiness, with the occasional tinge of absurd. Although I have not discussed this directly with him, I believe his haiku are deeply influenced by English, and particularly American, haiku traditions. Simon's work truly echoes Pound's Imagist poetry as well as the broader American haiku movement.

An additional notable distinction in Simon's haiku is the Zen-like quality embedded in his work. His poems frequently capture fleeting moments of insight and intuition, aligning with the perspective D.T. Suzuki (1870–1966) expressed in his book "Zen Buddhism and Its Influence on Japanese Culture" (1938). Suzuki argued that the essence of Zen lies in grasping moments of enlightenment, and he regarded haiku as the ideal medium for conveying such insights. Suzuki's linking of haiku with Zen laid the foundation for later interpretations of haiku in English-speaking cultures as being intrinsically tied to Zen philosophy. Reading Simon's poetry collection, one cannot help but notice how he captures profound moments of connection with nature, moments that evoke a subtle yet unmistakable sense of Zen. Through his work, Simon reveals the beauty of transient insights, inviting readers to pause, reflect, and embrace the delicate interplay between nature and the human experience.

Simon is a European, Southern Italian poet living in Shenzhen, an international metropolis in China — a true poet. From what I know, see, hear, and experience, he is also the most active poet in Shenzhen (without exception). Poetry to him is as essential as food or, perhaps more aptly, as Chinese tea (if my observations are correct, the word tea appears four times in this collection, and in life, he is deeply immersed in the world of tea culture).

Beyond tea, his poetry naturally contains more significant Chinese elements, possibly thanks to a "partner in crime"— his wife, Jiaomei Liu. This haiku collection includes imagery such as Guanyin, Shenzhen elements, and Shenzhen architecture (e.g., the Ping'an Tower). However, the most profound Chinese influence is the classical philosophy of the unity of heaven and humanity. Simon's poems often convey a deep, far-reaching aesthetic, expressing a fusion of human civilization and natural landscapes, where the self dissolves into the scene. His poetry touches on Buddhism (Zen being one of its major branches, flourishing in Japan), Christianity, and Taoism. As a haiku-focused collection, seasonal references (kigo) are naturally indispensable. Many poems use local plants or explicit terms to represent the seasons. But Simon also skilfully employs personification, metaphor, and other literary devices from Western poetic traditions.

If I were to define Simon Chiatante, I would call him an "urban romanticist". He is someone who lives the city, yet constantly finds connections with nature, communicates with it, and establishes a harmonious and beautiful relationship between humanity and the natural world — the flowers, the sun, the moon (which appears six times). This beautiful relationship is often captured in fleeting or transient moments of "Respiro": and is this not precisely the theme of the collection?

Silent urban nights —
A lily blooms unnoticed,
The city exhales.

Prof. Zhang Guangkui
Shenzhen University
January 5, 2025

Respiro

How often
Does a poet die
At sunset

Quante volte
Un poeta muore
Al tramonto

A wasp
Stopped, staring at me.
October 11th

Una vespa
Si ferma, guardandomi.
Undici ottobre

Hills still dreaming,
Morning mists dissolving
Slowly, slowly

Le colline sognano
Ancora, la nebbia si dissolve
Lenta, lenta

Careful steps
Under the heavy rain
What tomorrow?

Passi attenti
Sotto la pioggia battente
What tomorrow?

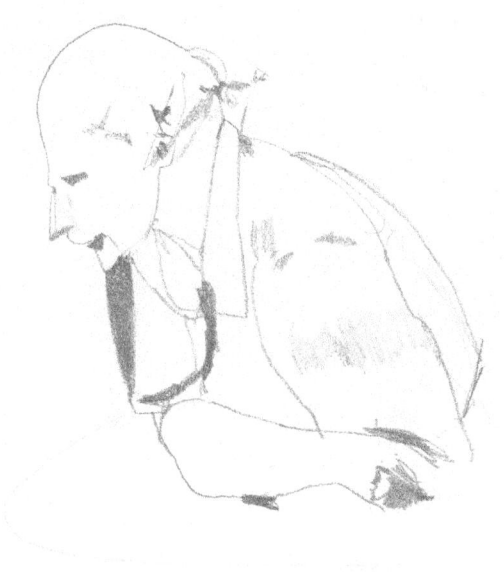

Stubborn
Skylark, enjoying
The rains of May

*L'allodola
Cocciuta, si gode
Le pioggie di maggio*

Spring rain
The first note
Of the Guqin

*Pioggia
Di primavera, il suono
Di una cetra*

Night storms
Mingle with the dreams.
Morning is calm

Tempeste
Intersecano i sogni.
Quieta la mattina

Flowers in the noodles shop
Respiro
Cities of the South

Fiori nel ristorante cinese
Respiro
Città del meridione

Ping An tower
Re-emerging from
White nothing

Il grattacielo
Di Ping An riemerge
Dal bianco nulla

Sospeso
Between the crowds
And the clouds

Suspensus
Tra le folle
E le nuvole

Come by the window,
Tonight
The moon is at its biggest

Vieni alla finestra,
Stanotte
La luna è così grande

White laundry
Hangs translucent
Against the moonlight

La biancheria
Appesa è illuminata
Dalla luna

L'inizio nella fine
Congregated soundscapes
Beneath the city sky

Principium in fine est
Aggregati sonori
Sotto il cielo della città

Long titanic bridges
After midnight
The sky's a silken brocade

Titanici
Ponti a mezzanotte, il cielo
È un broccato di seta

Heavy on their million
Screens
Like these lilies in the dew

Pesanti sui loro mille
Schermi
Come gigli di rugiada

This gentle wind
Caressing mosaics
Of distant window-lights

Questo vento
Accarezza mosaici
Finestre lontane

Past heaps of tenements
Azure layers
Of hills clouds skies

Oltre i palazzi
Fasci azzurri di colline
Nuvole, cieli

Singularity —
Extension/post dejavu
Text.style

Singolarità —
Extension/post dejavu
Text.style

Framing
The corners of my vision,
Morning glories

Ipomoea purpurea
Abbraccia
Il mio scenario

The wisteria's budding again
She kept saying
With these waves of heat

Il glicine sta fiorendo
Di nuovo diceva
Con queste ondate di caldo

Midway,
The clouds still
Hanging low

A metà strada
Le nuvole aspettano
Basse, ancora

Great herons
Across great golden
Clouds

Grandi aironi
Tra grandi
Nuvole d'oro

Fading sunrays
In an empty kindergarten
On Sunday evening

Declinano i raggi
Della domenica sera
In un asilo vuoto

Abandoned mall
At dusk, truth
And times inter-are

Centro abbandonato
Nel crepuscolo, attraverso
Tempi e verità

An opening
In the thicket, far towers
In construction

Un'apertura
Tra gli alberi, torri lontane
In costruzione

Softer than an island,
A hilltop
From the clouds

Una collina
Piú morbida di un'isola
Sulle nuvole

Capture the
Incalculable – intersection
Observer ((entries))

Catturare
L'incalcolabile – intersection
Observer ((entries))

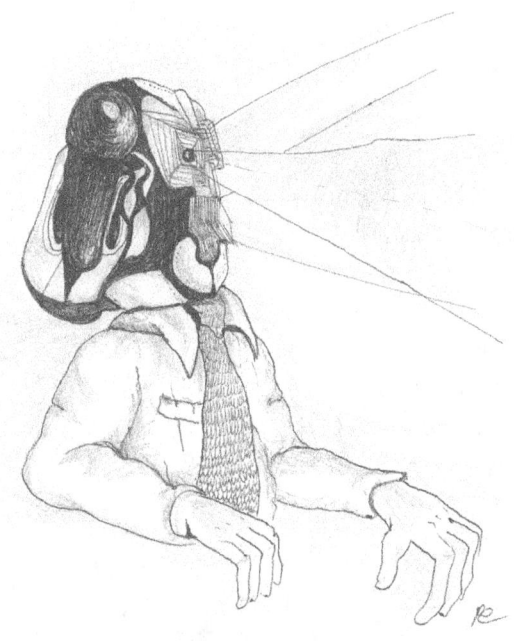

Criss cross
Speeding bikes beside
The empty teashop

Criss cross
Motorette elettriche
Per la sala da tè

Polyphonic
Inconsistencies linked
Between barriers

Per barriere
Condotte incongruenze
Polifoniche

Database
Is buffering with
The lilies

– Caricamento –
Insieme al database
E i gigli

Thrown in the bushes
A letter
With red corrections

Buttata nei cespugli
C'è una lettera
Corretta a penna rossa

Envisioning
– error – the future with
Art – gaps – vehicle

Visualizzando
– errore – il futuro dall
Arte – gaps – veicolo

Tired hoard
Upon this lifelong
Escalator

Stanca orda
Sopra queste scale lunghe
Una vita

Don't frown upon
These lines
Of senseless winds

Non far smorfie
A questi versi
Di vento insensibile

I forgot
What to say — rises
A crimson moon

Ho perso
Il filo — ma sorge
La luna rossa

Momentary
Dharma
Bamboo in a pot

Bambú in una teiera
Dharma
Momentaneo

Finding
Your own silence
After the rainstorm

Dopo la tempesta
Ritrovando
Il proprio silenzio

Three broken
Watches in a drawer, unknown
Sanctuary of time

Tre orologi rotti
In un cassetto, sconosciuto
Santuario del tempo

School wall,
Setting yellow buds
Over the vine

Il muro della scuola
Brilla di boccioli gialli
Sopra i ceppi

Noonshine
Silenzio e solitudine —
The city naps

Silentium et solitudo
Al meriggiare
La città riposa

From silence
Blossoming — the shy student
Raised his hand

Fiorire
Nel silenzio — alza la mano
Il timido studente

Under the trees
The street corner barber
Busier than ever

All'ombra degli alberi
Il barbiere da strada
Più impegnato che mai

This difficult beauty
Of gnarled roots
Across the concrete

La bellezza difficile
Di radici
Contorte nel cemento

Just a wall
Not four, no roof,
In the fields

Solo un muro
Non quattro, non un tetto
In mezzo ai campi

Fire burnt clouds
Just
As they call them

Nuvole di fiamma
Cosí
Come le chiamano

Silk, yarn, even Ghazals
Harbor
In these placid bays

Anche Ghazal approdano
Con sete e filari
In queste baie placide

A palace of green
Fantasies
Sunlit primary school

Un palazzo di verdi
Fantasie
Una scuola al sole

Old mall's long gone
Days of splendor, fallen
Tiger lilies

Cadono i gigli tigre
I giorni passati di splendore
Vecchi negozi chiusi

Silent
Meeting her
— Autumn drizzle

Appuntamento
In silenzio — pioviggina
In autunno

It's still here
The seafood restaurant
We never tried

Il ristorante di pesce
Che non abbiamo mai provato
È ancora li

Poetry
Walking through
A rainfall

Poesia
Passi nella
Pioggia

Gate of the old park,
Green aura
Beside the city street

Verde aura
La porta del vecchio parco
Su una strada di città

At the park's gate
With the crickets, leaving
The world behind

All'entrata del parco
Con i grilli, lasciandomi
Il mondo alle spalle

Forlorn
A Guanyin's bust
— Falling leaves

Derelitto
Busto di madonna
— Foglie al vento

Suddenly the trees
Started whispering
At the Taoist shrine

Ad un tratto
Gli alberi sussurrarono
Al tempio taoista

From the wild
Park's recesses, to a
Private garden

Da un angolo remoto
Del parco naturale
A un giardino privato

Enhanced
By raindrops, the blossoms
Of the narcissus

Magnificati
Dalla pioggia i boccioli
Del narciso

Just like
An ancient turtle
— River stone

Un'antica
Tartaruga
O una pietra di fiume

Far
From home
The koel's song

*Lontano
Da casa, il canto
Del cuculo*

Across
Mysterious paths
— Roselle hibiscus

Tra sentieri
Misteriosi
— Roselle hibiscus

Dreams of
Absolute necessity
The heavy rain

Sogni di necessità
Assoluta — la pioggia
Battente

Father and son
Without a word, hiding
From the storm

Padre e figlio
Al riparo dalla tempesta
In silenzio

Abissi
Charging towards us,
These leaden clouds

Barathra
Marciano verso di noi
Queste nuvole di piombo

Sailing
On a petal
How carefree

Navigando
Su di un petalo
Che libertà

Lonely crane
A river far, far
Away

Solitaria gru
Un fiume lontano
Lontano

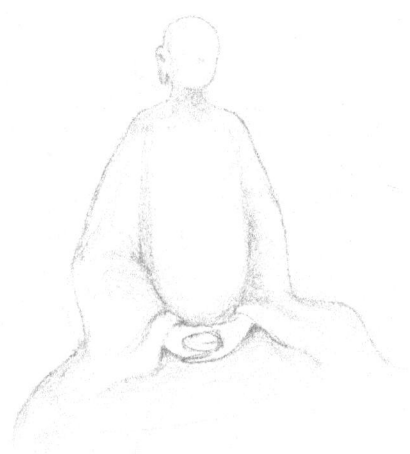

A river
Of one kind, eventually
Absence

*Un solo
Fiume, infine
Assenza*

Beside me
On the marble sill
— The full moon

Di fianco a me
Sul davanzale di marmo
— La luna piena

Scent of lilies
Under the full moon,
The mind is focused

Concentrato
Alla luce della luna,
L'odore dei gigli

Contemplating
Daruma, I over brew
The tea

Nel contemplare
Daruma
Il tè mi è uscito amaro

Sutra
Bell, dispersed
In all directions

La campana del sutra
Si disperde
In ogni direzione

At the end
Of the year, the tea
Is tasteless

Alla fine
Dell'anno, il tè
Non ha sapore

Grass
And roses — clouds
On the teapot

Rose
Verzura — nuvole
Sopra la teiera

Gold
On laquer — ancient
Dreams

Oro
Su nera lacca — sogni
Antichi

On the way
To say goodbye,
The moonset

Sulla via
Per dirsi addio
Cala la luna

Night shrine
Its open doors
To the late traveler

Santuario di notte
Le porte sono aperte
Per il tardo viaggiatore

Once
Jade, gold and attendants
Now, one stranger

C'erano una volta
Giada, oro e servitú
Ora, uno straniero

No gold
No shrine, no one
Under this tree

Niente oro
Né santuari, nessuno
Sotto quest'albero

Cicada's tusk,
But I still hear
Its song

Della cicala
Solo le zampe ma io
Ne sento il canto

Stone paths
Lost beneath
The vines

Sentieri
Di pietra perduti
Tra i vitigni

The magpies'
Croak — speeds up
The falling leaf

Gracchiano
Le gazze — cade
Una foglia veloce

Like constellations
Tiny flowers
In the autumnal grass

Costellazioni
Come fiori
Nell'erba autunnale

Citrus
Scented breeze
On empty hills

Agrumata
Brezza
Sopra vacue colline

Forgotten
Tomb by the roadside
— Birds only

Una tomba
Dimenticata sul sentiero
— Passeri soli

A tiny wren
Is chanting by the
Forlorn Buddha

Canta
Uno scricciolo vicino
Al Buddha

Fresh
Vegetables — old
Old man

Un uomo vecchio
Vecchio — verdura
Fresca

Broken bricks
Of an old well.
The banyan roots

Radici di banyan
Mattoni rotti
Di un vecchio pozzo

The rain stopped
Evening crickets
By the lake

Ferma la pioggia
I grilli
La sera al lago

Curtains, and outside
The pampas
In one single wave

Tende,
Come un'onda
I ciuffi delle canne

On his deathbed
Smiling
About the sea

Sul letto di morte
Sorride
Pensando al mare

A fly
In my soup
— Keep eating

Un moscerino
Nella zuppa
— Continua a mangiare

Cold days
The leeks on the sill
Grow twisted

Con il freddo
I porri sul davanzale
Crescono storti

Shawl shrouded
Angel sitting
On the desert's rim

Un angelo siede avvolto
Da uno scialle
Ai confini del deserto

Eyes low
Faint smiles — from sands
To the metropolis

Occhi bassi
Lieve sorriso — dalle sabbie
Alla metropoli

Merak —
Sipping quietly
At a crossroads

Merak —
Sorseggiando calmo
Ad un incrocio

Ages
Of mist — the slopes
Have reappeared

Epoche di nebbia —
Riappaiono
I pendii

Intersections
Of wrong translations
And the hills behind

Si intersecano
Inesatte traduzioni
E le colline

We dream
Polygonal
— Hazy skyline

Sogniamo
Poligonali
— Indistinti orizzonti

The view
Below is made of
Crystal

La vista
Dall'alto
È di cristallo

Too late
For cherry blossoms.
Memories in bloom

Tardi
Per i fiori di ciliegio.
Sbocciano i ricordi

Hovering above
The empty streets at noon,
Jasmines

Aleggiano
Al meriggio sulle strade
Vuote, gelsomini

Slow suburban
Afternoon, under drowsy
Tall tenements

Tra palazzi alti
Di periferia, un pomeriggio
Lento, tiepido

Crosslegged in front
Of artificial intelligence
Installations

Padmasana
Seduto di fronte a istallazioni
Di intelligenza artificiale

Imagined
Cherry blossoms
As barb wires

Immagini
Boccioli di ciliegio
Filo spinato

Symmetrical
City — waving
Palm leaves

Simmetrica
Città — ondeggiano
Le palme

The summer's sunrise
Doubled
On the old man's glasses

Si raddoppia l'alba
Estiva
Negli occhiali di quell'uomo

Flickering
Like flames across masses
In the morning rush

Tremolanti
Fiammelle tra le masse
La mattina

Gate gate paragate —
Wherever this train is
Taking us

Gate gate paragate —
Ovunque ci conduca
Questo treno

The Ecology of Self

Does language make us special? Is language a fingerprint of our environment? Does language influence our evolution?

One of the most striking features of human cognition is the ability to generate an infinite number of meanings by combining a finite set of words and constructs, aggregated through syntax and imagination, linking our history with the present environment and emotions. This ability is most evident in language, a reflection of environmental intelligence; but it also characterizes other aspects of our cognition, such as drawing, computation, and music, regardless of our intentionality.

Chiatante's haiku flood the mind with a variety of emotions, driven by their modern and varied structure. Although short, these haiku convey a vibrancy of color, form, texture, and rhythm — the essence of each perceiving soul. The environment, waterscapes and urban landscapes, dominate this self-expression as an exploration of the self. The ecology of haiku, represented by the interconnectedness of words and punctuation, is a free form, deviating from canonical standards yet giving an innovative form to an impulsive writing of feelings. What we sense from the environment, what we feel to communicate, is central to our connection with others, with the world.

Despite our conscious rationality, in Chiatante's haiku there is a silent but perceptible voice, perhaps unframed but unconsciously consistent, that wants to communicate experiences through the passion for the medium of words. A voice through drops of water, storms, shrines, moons, urban spaces, herons and chickens, children and smiles, trees and shopping malls, cups and bread, Italian and English, girl and woman, day and night. It feels like a painting in which memories of oneself, of the reader, merge with the description of Chiatante's whereabouts, physical and emotional, in Shenzhen, mixing Chinese and Western elements: the hydrography, or "ecography" in a broader sense, as the blueprint of our environment and of inspired words. A passion for words, sadly disappearing in our world, yet so critical to human connection and universal across media. A fabric of words that aims at self-reflection; an organizer; a desire to live unknown feelings and experiences; and a communicator to enter the souls of others and connect with them: this is the power of the ecology of words — the ability to connect and influence.

Whatever future we believe in or try to construct, words will always be the core of our intelligence, our humanity, which we cannot neglect. And Chiatante's haiku are pleasant to read whenever we want to escape from the reality we find ourselves in and explore it, gently conjuring in our minds the images conveyed by his words: whether while riding the subway, lying in a park, or wherever we feel like being. Words as waves of emotion, waves of adventure, waves of freedom. The waving fabric of beautiful words as a testament to our collective being.

Matteo Convertino
Professor in Ecosystem Design and Engineering
fuTuRE EcoSystems Lab
Tsinghua University, Shenzhen International Graduate School

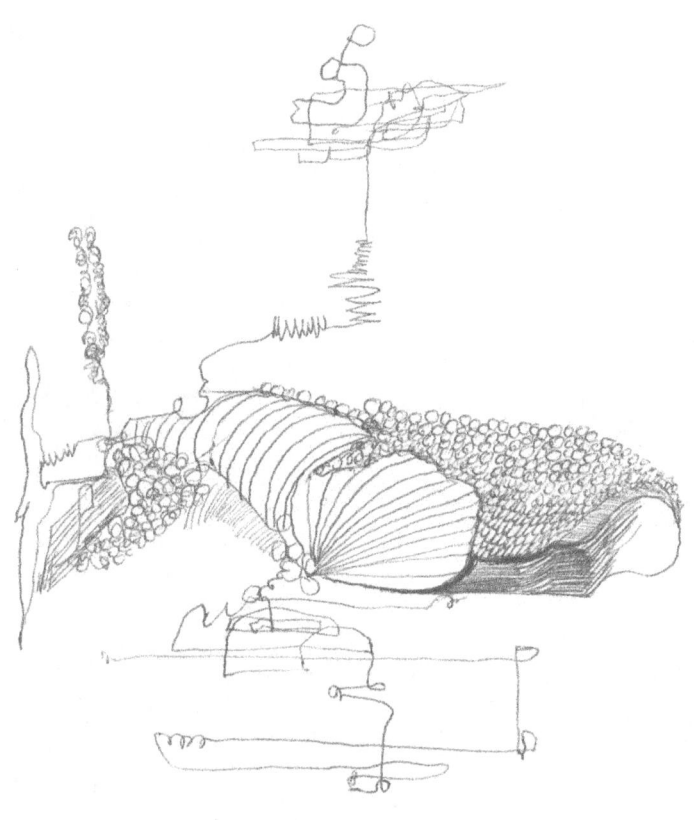

AFTERWORD: THE ECOLOGY OF SELF

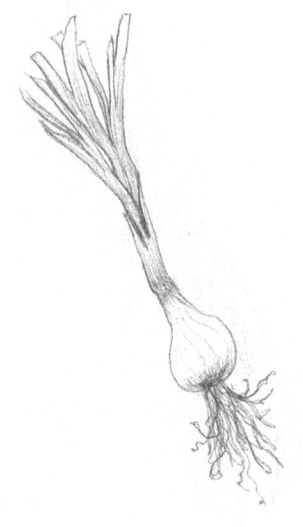

~~Questo~~
Haiku non è
~~Un haiku~~

~~This~~
~~Haiku is not~~
~~A haiku—~~

www.ingramcontent.com/pod-product-compliance
Lightning Source LLC
LaVergne TN
LVHW052340080426
835508LV00045B/3103